KENGO KUMA: PORTLAND JAPANESE GARDEN

KENGO KUMA: PORTLAND JAPANESE GARDEN

Written and edited by
Botond Bognár and Balázs Bognár

Introduction by Kengo Kuma

Designed by Takaaki Matsumoto

First published in the United States of America in 2019 by
Rizzoli Electa
A Division of
RIZZOLI INTERNATIONAL PUBLICATIONS, INC.
300 Park Avenue South, New York, NY 10010
www.rizzoliusa.com

ISBN-13: 978-0-8478-6466-9
Library of Congress Control Number: 2018962109

Distributed to the U.S. Trade by Random House, New York

Designed by Takaaki Matsumoto, Matsumoto Inc.

Printed and bound in China

2021 2022 2023 2024 2025 / 10 9 8 7 6 5 4 3

Front endpapers: The upper pond in the Strolling Pond Garden, showing also the
Moon Bridge, in full autumn colors. Photo: Wayne Williams
Back side of front endpapers: The Heavenly Falls at the lower pond of the Strolling
Pond Garden in late spring. Photo: Patricia Reynolds
Back endpapers: Colorful carp (koi) in the Lower Pond of the Strolling Pond
Garden. Photo: Tyler Quinn
Back side of back endpapers: A close up view of the 85-year-old weeping cherry tree
in the Flat Garden. Photo: Tyler Quinn
Frontispiece: The Umami Café perched over the steep terrain, as seen from the
original ticketing gate to the Garden. Photo: James Florio

Table of Contents

The Portland Japanese Garden, Portland, Oregon, with its extended new facilities of the Cultural Village and its new programs, is a truly exceptional example of a Japanese garden and cultural institution today. Its special character is primarily the result of how it pursues its mission, which takes it far beyond fulfilling the typical role of Japanese gardens as venues for personal enjoyment, communion with nature, contemplation, spiritual healing, and finding inner peace. Although meeting all these on an unusually high level of artistry, the Portland Japanese Garden also plays a greatly expanded role; it has established and leads the new International Japanese Garden Training Center and is committed to the training of current and future gardeners. Moreover, the organization extends its educational offering beyond professional practitioners to the general public about traditional gardening and various other aspects of Japanese culture: tea ceremony, flower arrangement, haiku poetry, and many others. It achieves this by teaching both techniques and aesthetics through total immersion and not just by demonstration. The Garden also organizes various performances, lectures, and exhibitions. Many instructors and performers are invited from Japan directly, whereas other Japan-inspired artists arrive from around the world. In these aims, the facilities, both the Garden and the buildings, are instrumental, insofar as they serve as concrete examples to study.

The compilation of this monograph is similarly unusual. First, it was clear at the outset that in this case it is not merely the Cultural Village that is new; it is the entire Portland Japanese Garden that is new, both as an actual place and as an institution altogether, even though the original gardens remain unchanged. What has changed, however, is that it can be experienced only together with the added elements of architecture and new landscaping, as the Garden has expanded to nearly twice of its original size. In other words, the symbiotic relationship between the new and the old alters them both and arguably for the better. It is this kind of *tsunagu* (relationship) and its long-developed and time-tested Japanese artistic conjuring that we had to elucidate as essential in order to better understand the significance of the new Portland Japanese Garden. Accordingly, in addition to detailed discussions of the existing Garden and the new Cultural Village, we have included concise introductions to such topics as the crucial role of nature in Japanese culture, the art of gardens and architecture in Japan, the artistry of Kengo Kuma's architecture in general, as well as, very importantly, the craftsmanship that was invested in the design and construction of the Cultural Village. It is our hope that these expanded if unconventional inclusions will help both the reader of this monograph and the visitor to the Portland Japanese Garden in their explorations and learning.

—The Authors

The Entry Garden and the Antique Gate with the illuminated Cultural Village above the wooded hill cloaked in early morning autumn fog

7

Introduction

The day I first visited the Portland Japanese Garden was unforgettable. I had never experienced a garden in Japan like this. Yet, there was no mistaking that it was a Japanese garden. Nestled beneath the canopy of an Oregon forest of giant cedar and cypress trees unlike anything in Japan, this special garden hides quietly as if it were "buried." Its creator, Dr. Takuma Tono, who, after graduating from Hokkaido Agriculture University, studied the American genre of landscape at Cornell University, belonged neither to Japan nor to the United States: it was as if he had the unique ability to live in a special nongravitational space between these two places and cultures. It was from this in-between realm that he was able to design this exceptional garden in Portland. By composing the Portland Japanese Garden as an unusual combination of four styles, each from a different period, he managed to make them coexist and at the same time to separate them based on their differences in ground level.

Just as Dr. Tono had done with the Garden, I wanted to create a special architecture and place that also did not belong solely to either culture; it would be neither entirely American nor completely Japanese. To put it another way, the place I intended to conjure up through my design had to be adequately both Japanese and American. After visiting Portland, I had the strong feeling that the local citizens loved and praised this kind of quality represented by the Garden. My interaction with Stephen D. Bloom, the CEO of the Garden, convinced me about this even more.

9

The world needs such a place that unites. Why? Because, on the one hand the world has started to divide and the differences are growing; on the other hand, people are becoming all the more intolerant of one another. For this very reason, a place like the Portland Japanese Garden is necessary. Now, more than ever, the world needs a place that lies between countries and cultures, while accepting and upholding them equally.

—Kengo Kuma

The Cultural Village nestled among the magnificent and colorful Douglas firs and western red cedars in late autumn sunshine

Reverence of Nature and Japanese Culture

Mountains, rivers, all things living
pay homage to the whims of the seasons
in their eternal cycle—Seisei

It is an accepted notion that the origin of any culture is rooted in a particular group of people's observance of, or more precisely, interaction with its environment: topographic and climatic conditions, the variety of flora and

fauna, that is to say the land and *nature*. From this interaction springs the distinctive makeup of beliefs and knowledge, customs or rituals, values and religion, language, arts, the ways and means of building or shaping the human environment, and many other features that characterize a given culture; one might say, culture outlines reality and articulates the meaning of life.

If this holds true in general, it is even more so in the case of Japan. The country, consisting of four main islands and

Mt. Fuji seen from the south

thousands of smaller ones, is blessed with an exceptional richness of natural beauty. The seashore is not only long but also attractively varied. About 80 percent of the land is covered by ranges of high mountains, which can be

both dramatic and, with much of them forested and verdant, picturesque. Many among these are volcanoes. Although some, like Mount Fuji, are dormant, many others are active, and seismic activity is also frequent. Stretching a great distance from southwest toward northeast, the country experiences a broad range of climatic conditions. It has four seasons, yet, as the Japanese identify the two rainy seasons of the shifting monsoons (*tsuyu*) separately, the number rises to six. Owing to these wet

above: Cherry blossoms in full bloom within the Meguro Campus of Tokyo Institute of Technology in late March *left:* The Japanese Inland Sea seen with Naoshima Island *following pages:* Rice paddies in Yufuin Village of Oita Prefecture

seasons, Japan benefits from ample precipitation; the land is fertile and lush in greenery.

Throughout their long history, the Japanese have developed an acute sensibility to their environment. This has been fostered on the one hand by frequent devastating typhoons and earthquakes and on the other by the

11

Crowd visiting the Ise Shinto shrine Naiku compound on the occasion of its 62nd rebuilding in 2013

The large bronze Buddha statue, the Daibutsu in Todai-ji Temple of Nara (752 AD)

above: A part of Ise Shrine Naiku compound
left: Father and son "listening" to a sacred tree on the way to the Ise Shinto shrine Naiku compound

laboriousness of rice production on the available land, which has always been limited by the geography of the country. In other words, nature was at once bountiful, harsh, and unpredictable, but the livelihood of people depended on it. Thus, despite the hardships and limitations, or perhaps because of them, a keen adaptation to and more importantly deep appreciation of nature have been nurtured since ancient times giving birth to Shinto, the indigenous system of beliefs or mythology of Japan.

Shinto, meaning "the way of the gods," is a pantheistic, non-exclusive, quasi religion, which has no founder or doctrines nor any sacred texts. Its animism recognizes divinity in every attribute of nature, organic and inorganic, according to which particular deities, called kami, could inhabit mountains, rocks and islands, trees, as well as ancestors, and the Emperor himself. The more special the form or position of the things (*go-shintai*) or persons, the more divine and venerated they are. The Sun Goddess, or *Amaterasu Omi-kami*, has been worshipped as the most sacred one, as she represents the origin of Japan, the Land of the Rising Sun, and its people, the Japanese. Yet, it is important to point out that in kami there is nothing similar to the transcendent deities of Western religions. Shinto is rooted in the observance and celebration of the cyclical changes in nature, as well as of the concrete phenomena in rhythmical daily life and human existence.

Shinto survived and flourished even after Buddhism was introduced into Japan from China in about the sixth century. Advocating the illusory nature of reality while intending to transcend it through a conduct toward spiritual enlightenment (satori or nirvana), Buddhism had a more sophisticated outlook on the world. Although rather different from Shinto's affirmative stance on life, Buddhism in its claim of "all things must pass," recognizes the evanescence and impermanence of every existence. Thus, Buddhism betrays some similarities to the tenets of Shinto, which lack any notion of absolutes. Both belief systems are devoid of the strict dualism of the West. Opposing elements or qualities, like yin and yang, are linked as they mutually define each other, and either of the two can even be transformed into the other through human intervention or the performance of certain rituals. In their symbiotic relationship, Shinto and Buddhism have throughout the centuries continued to shape the ethos of Japanese life and culture, including the strong admiration of, and inspiration by, nature and its phenomenal world.

Shinto shrines have been built in devotion to the divine spirits of unique places and phenomena. This way, shrines often served also as "landmarks" of some exceptional manifestations of nature. There are innumerable smaller and larger shrines all over Japan, each for a different kami. The most sacred shrine is dedicated to *Amaterasu*, the Sun Goddess. Located in Ise, within a deep forest of Mie Prefecture, it is rebuilt every twenty years to provide a fresh abode for the deity. This ritual of rebuilding signifies also the cyclical changes in nature and the renewal of both place and time. To date, it has been reconstructed 62 times, the last being in 2013. As most shrines were built in remote areas, they are approached via long and intricate passages (*sandō*) along a sequence of many checkpoints, such as torii gates, stone lanterns (*dōrō* or *tōrō*), and drinking fountains, on the way to the sacred compound. The prolonged journey provides worshippers with the experience of nature and the psychological preparation or purification for their arrival at the shrine. Here the journey to the shrine is as important as, if not more so, than the actual arrival.

One of the several Torii Gates along the way to the Naiku compound of Ise shrine

Japanese art, too, is deeply indebted to the intimate relationship of the Japanese to nature and the passing of time. Flower arrangement (ikebana), landscape in a planter or tray (bonsai and bon-seki), tea ceremony (chanoyu), pottery (*yakimono*), black ink painting (sumi-e), calligraphy (*shodo*), the traditional poetry (haiku), woodblock prints (ukiyo-e), decorative arts, and so many others, are all born in the spirit of the phenomenal world and the sense of "here and now." Japanese art suggests but does not confirm; it is situational and often ambiguous, inciting human imagination and interpretation. The term "*mono-no-aware*" expresses the Japanese artist's much appreciated sensitivity to ephemera. As the historian and architect Tomoya Masuda observed, the Japanese are interested in "delicate earthly changes rather than heavenly permanence," and this spirit has, *naturally*, imbued the inception of both architecture and gardens.

right: The tunnel-like hiking trail under "thousands" of closely-paced red Torii (*Senbon Torii*) gates in the Fushimi Inari Shinto shrine (seventeenth century) of Kyoto
following pages: Paintings of bamboo groves and other scenes of nature on the sliding shoji panels in Nanzen-ji Temple of Kyoto (1611)

Architecture and Gardens in Japan

The garden in Japan cannot be treated independently of architecture.
—Günter Nitschke. *Japanese Gardens*

家庭

The Chinese characters (*kanji*) of "household" or *Katei*, where *ka* means "building" or "house" and *tei* "garden," refers to the unity of architecture and garden or nature

Tiny *tsubo niwa* within the interior of a traditional urban residence (*machiya*) in the fishing village of Yanai, Yamaguchi Prefecture

left: The Shokin-tei tea pavilion within the compound of Katsura Imperial Villa (seventeenth century) blends into the landscape of the famous stroll garden (*kaiyu shiki teien*)

Without doubt, Japanese architecture has developed in response to, or rather, in close and intimate relationship with nature. Buildings were created as organic parts of their environment both literally and figuratively. This was assured by the builders' acute sensitivity to siting and to the natural materials used: wood, bamboo, straw, paper, thatch, slate, and some stone, and by means of the builders' artful articulation of a variable spatial continuity between architecture and the landscape. However, the landscape— that is to say nature—has almost always been represented by gardens. The inseparable coexistence of architecture and gardens in Japanese culture is expressed also by the word for "household" (*ka-tei*), which is the combination of the characters for house *and* garden. Yet, these gardens were not simply small parts of the self-grown and existing landscape; they were *not* natural. They have always been a kind of nature that humans produced and cultivated within the confines of artificial enclosures, and they could vary in both size and type.

However, regardless of which ones are considered: the miniscule courtyard gardens (*tsubo niwa*), the small rock gardens (*kare-sansui*), the simple, moss-covered tea gardens (*chaniwa*), then the larger stroll or landscape gardens, often with ponds (*kaiyushiki niwa*), or any others, each one was conceived of as a specific representation of the world or the universe. Indeed, gardens came to be microcosms that corresponded aesthetically as well as philosophically to the universe; such a macrocosm might be that of the natural world, what the Japanese tried to understand and imagine, or the kind they wished it to be, like paradise. As Japanologist Günter Nitschke put it, "The history of Japanese garden is the history of man's search for his place within nature and thereby, ultimately, his search for himself." In this

The buildings in Ginkaku-ji Temple of Kyoto (1480)
"disappear" in the surrounding landscape garden

e Kenroku-en garden with the celebrated two-legged
ne lantern (*kotoji-toro*) in Kanazawa, Ishikawa Prefecture

left: The upper stroll garden (*kaiyu shiki teien*) of Shugaku-in Imperial Villa in Kyoto (seventeenth century) with the borrowed scenery (*shakkei*) of mountains in the background

following pages, left: The Urakuen tea garden featuring one of Japan's three finest teahouses (*chashitsu*), the Jo-an (in the background) by Oda Urakusai, in Inuyama, Aichi Prefecture (originally from Kyoto, 1618)

following pages, right: The renowned dry-landscape (*kare-sansui*) or rock garden of Ryoan-ji Zen Temple (1488) in Kyoto

process throughout the centuries, garden design in Japan has been elevated on to an extremely sophisticated, high level of art.

The origin of Japanese gardens can be traced back to the simple, white pebbled and empty courtyards of ancient Shinto shrines, as seen at Ise (third century), but pebbled and graveled surfaces have remained important elements of later gardens as well. By the early seventeenth century three major types of gardens evolved and reached their peak. Laid out along intricate paths, stroll or landscape gardens, usually parts of the estates of aristocrats and feudal lords, daimyo, came to be delicate aggregates of numerous episodic sceneries. Lacking in any geometric pattern, they unfold through alternating turns (*oremagari*) in a "hide-and-seek" (*miegakure*) manner, revealing endless layers of unexpected vistas that often reference actual Japanese landscapes. Yet, when possible, these gardens also borrow sceneries (*shakkei*) from the outside, like views of rivers, remote hills or mountains, and so on, to include in their compositions. While the elements or parts—for example, groups of trees and shrubs, rocks, mounds, stepping-stones, small bridges over ponds,

Viewing the garden from the veranda (*engawa*) of Koto-in Zen Temple (1603) in Kyoto

and tiny islands—are presented in immediacy and in sharp focus, the totality or the whole of their world remains nebulous and imaginary, thus open to a wide variety of interpretations. Usually, as these gardens are recalled in memory, they appear to be larger than their actual size.

As Zen and its practice of tea—both introduced from China—reached popularity after the twelfth century, two additional main types of garden began to develop in Japan. Since Zen advocates meditation, these gardens serve as vehicles toward that goal. The approaching path (*roji*) to the temple or the teahouse (*chashitsu* or *sōan*), hidden deep within the wooded garden, is not only long but, with all distracting elements like bright colors eliminated, also simple and serene. The floor among the trees and other plants in the garden is damp and often carpeted with moss (*koke*). Yet, Zen gardens regularly feature ponds and islands as well which were considered divine. On the other hand, Zen rock gardens were designed as "dry landscapes" (*kare-sansui*). Confined by walls within rather limited spaces, they were not meant to be walked in, but only to be looked upon. Their severely minimalist and abstract composition of merely a few carefully selected and placed rocks within fine, raked white gravel—and some areas of moss—conjures up a curious realm of absence. Absorbing the sight, the meditating person is expected to gain insight into the state of

right: The *engawa*, an intermediary space between inside and outside, at the Koto-in Zen temple (1603) in Kyoto

emptiness, the sense of that *void* which Buddhism, particularly Zen, considers as inherent in all existence. In other words, these gardens symbolize *no-thing*. Writing about the one at Ryoan-ji Temple of 1488 in Kyoto, which represents

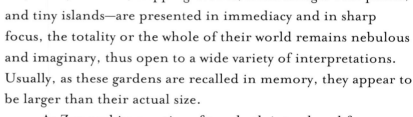

The double-layered *engawa* overlooking the rock garden
of Nanzen-ji Zen Temple in Kyoto (1611)

right: The garden around the Shisendo Villa of Kyoto
(1636) blends seamlessly with its interior when the outside,
light, sliding wall panels (fusuma) are fully opened

The interior of Yoshijima House (1881), the traditional
urban residence (*machiya*) of a well-to-do sake merchant
in Takayama, Gifu Prefecture, reveals the flexibly
layered system of shoji panels and the interconnected
fluid spaces they create

the sliding wall panels (fusuma and shoji)
…ned, one can see through the interior of the
…ken tea pavilion in the compound of Katsura
…erial Villa in Kyoto (seventeenth century)

the purest form of *kare-sansui* gardens in Japan, Nitschke noted "that it symbolizes *not*. . . . It belongs to the art of the void."

Gardens in Japan always coexist with the architecture they envelop or within which they are enclosed. Created as integral parts of gardens, buildings do not have a self-assertive authoritarian role. The symbiotic relationship between the two reached its artistic epitome in the refined and informal *sukiya-zukuri* residential architecture by the end of the sixteenth century. It developed as a fusion of the larger and more formal *shoin-zukuri* of the warrior class (samurai) and the small and rustic teahouses. *Sukiya* came to be the architecture of private residences and villas of the upper classes and Zen Buddhist monks but later, favored also by the general population, started to influence urban residences (*machiya*) and even rural farmhouses (*minka*). *Sukiya* is characterized by a sense of lightness and by its slim wood structural frame in modular design which is based on the size of the tatami mats inside. Equally important are *sukiya*'s thatch- or shingle-covered roofs with low and deep overhanging eaves above a system of surrounding wood verandas (*engawa*), as well as the light, translucent paper-covered sliding wall panels, which provide most of the outside enclosure (fusuma) and the inside partitions (shoji).

The mobility of these elements constitutes a remarkably flexible, layered spatial system. Depending on the disposition of the panels and various screens—bamboo reeds (*sudare*), split curtains (*noren*), and wood lattices (*kōshi*)—the exterior is allowed to gradually, though variably, penetrate deep into the interior, while the softly filtered light shifts toward varying shades of light and darkness. Yet, within larger, typically urban complexes tiny courtyard gardens, too, are inserted, facilitating some extra light and the presence of nature in miniature. Also inside, the display of ikebana, bonsai, scroll paintings, and haiku reference the seasons. The usual zigzag or "flying geese" (*gankō*) layout of buildings increases further the interface between architecture and nature. In this process, the intermediary space of the *engawa* plays a significant role; it renders the boundary of buildings soft and ambiguous, while architecture, becoming the transformed continuation of the garden, shuns monumentality. This architecture appeals not only with its elegant minimalism and its quiet and low-profile presence but also with its capacity to make the inhabitants feel they still live in the midst of nature.

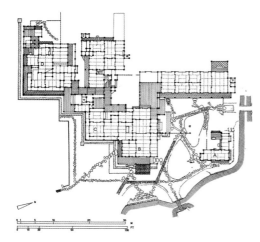

Floor plan of Katsura Imperial Villa in Kyoto (seventeenth century)

34

right: The zigzagging or "flying geese" (*gankō*) arrangement of the Katsura Imperial Villa in Kyoto (seventeenth century)

The Katsura Imperial Villa (seventeenth century) in Kyoto, shown with its outside sliding panels (fusuma) all closed

The Portland Japanese Garden

When creating a garden, let the exceptional work of past master gardeners be your guide. Heed the desires of the master of the house, yet heed as well one's own taste.—Excerpted from *Sakuteiki*

The path on the way to the Flat Garden and the Pavilion Gallery in autumn colors

At the tender age of 55 years, the Portland Japanese Garden has quietly become one of the world's foremost examples of the art of the Japanese garden. This is particularly astonishing given that it is not in Japan and not remotely as old as its counterparts there. Between its formal opening in 1967 and again with the new Cultural Village in 2017, a passionate grassroots effort transformed a nearly unsuitable site into a moving place of contemplation and appreciation for Japan's richly multifaceted aesthetics. Today, it finds itself at the helm of a greater mission to act as the leading international example for building similar garden-based catalysts for studying Japanese arts—a vigorous ambition with literal and cultural seeds in its relatively modest 12-acre territory.

A mere 15 years after the end of World War II, Portland initiated its sister city relationship with Sapporo in 1959 as a means of encouraging Oregonian interest in Japanese culture and renewing American links to Japan. Part of this was the burgeoning effort of the Japan-America Society of Oregon, in selecting a location for an authentic Japanese garden—a symbol of the vital, storied ties between the two countries. By 1960, with the significant support of Mayor Terry Schrunk and other civic leaders, the group identified its current location in Portland's West Hills area. While gardens in Japan tend to arise from Buddhist tradition, Portland's Garden was distinctly community-driven—a gesture of outreach and healing rather than introspective representation of philosophy.

The site then was not a garden at all, but the defunct former Washington Park Zoo. There was little to hint at the meditative but wildly popular landscapes that would eventually grow in the ensuing decades—a place of cultural understanding and natural wonder. According to historian

left: Stone-paved walkway in the Flat Garden

Bruce Taylor Hamilton, whose book *Human Nature: The Japanese Garden of Portland, Oregon* (1996) explains the beginnings of Portland Japanese Garden in great detail, "It took vision for those interested in creating a Japanese garden to commit themselves to the location; the abandoned zoo property was described as merely a rock pile." There was almost nothing there, save for—symbolically if coincidentally—a solitary Japanese maple. Its former life aside, this was a clean slate.

It was this blank canvas that a specially assembled Garden Commission offered to landscape architect Professor Takuma Tono, who with tremendous foresight would establish the foundational design for the Portland Japanese Garden. Tono was well regarded and a logical choice, given his respected academic reputation and recently completed gardens in the United States, coupled with his bicultural training at both Hokkaido and Cornell Universities. His hiring was decisive, and in 1963 Tono began designing the landscape.

Hidden stairway in the Natural Garden in spring. Photo: William Sutton

Tono primarily worked from Tokyo, but his time on-site was concentrated, and his designs remain generative, iconic works at the Garden. Via lucid and succinct drawings, he penned four of the five main gardens: The Flat Garden, The Strolling Pond Garden, the Tea Garden, and the Sand and Stone Garden. Aided by area landscapers, Tono personally shaped the character of each on-site—during intensive and often rain-drenched visits—using available vegetation, donated specimen trees, and local materials. These four gardens are core moments in the visitor's experience today.

Professor Tono's vision for the Garden was prescient, but assuming that it was a fixed template also ignores the nuanced contributions of the directors who succeeded him. The simplest reason is that nature, the very substance under each director's steady eye, is not at all static. Plants grow; weather shifts; seasons change. A garden's slow evolution can only be perceived with the patient passage of time. In gardening terms, the act of maintenance cannot merely replicate what came before.

Instead, the Portland Japanese Garden is a series of cumulative edits, each directorial assignment a layer of adjusting and enriching the course of Tono's framework. Eight garden directors in focused appointments—each appointed from Japan to maintain a direct lineage of cultural authenticity—brought careful changes spanning a short 25 years starting in 1968, each living on location to devote attention to the original concepts.

The first two directors brought the gardens from infancy to early growth. Kinya Hira was a Tono protégé who nurtured the Flat Garden and

right: Maple tree near the Tea Garden in autumn colors

the Sand and Stone Garden into more developed stages—often under the exacting supervision of Tono—and commenced pivotal work on the Strolling Pond Garden. Successor Hoichi Kurisu connected this pond to the Heavenly Falls with a meandering stream spilling into a spread of irises and an area for koi. His hand brought additional natural touches at the edges of the Tono designs, merging them into surroundings with stonework.

The next directors attended to areas that had remained underdeveloped. Outside of the first four designs, Tono also envisioned a fifth, a Moss Garden, which Hachiro Sakakibara transformed into what is now the Natural Garden. This is a carefully choreographed sleight of hand with its interwoven rivulets, stone, and carefully placed vegetation—precision nature. Successor Michio Wakui focused on entrances: a *machiai* waiting shelter for the Tea Garden as an appropriate preamble for the 1968 Tea House, as well as the landscape flanking the Antique Gate.

The following two directors strengthened the upkeep of the gardens, though again with thoughtful intervention and personality imbued into

Autumn colors in the Strolling Pond Garden showing the green roofs of the Cultural Village blending into the foliage of trees. Photo: Bruce Forster

the details. Masayuki Mizuno, whose methods emphasized the importance of pausing and pacing in both visitor experience and gardening work, formalized the Garden's maintenance philosophies. His was an understated approach that introduced accents, benches, and intermediate moments to stitch the gardens together. Kichiro Sano took his tasks as various soft adjustments and upgrades, including the addition of demure waterfalls at the Strolling Pond Garden, revisions to the edges of the Natural Garden's pond, and continued development of the Tea Garden.

With continued subtlety, the final two directors completed the major ideas of Tono. Takao Donuma finished last phases of work on the Natural Garden and introduced traditional fencing to balance defined borders and spatial indeterminacy. Toru Tanaka replaced him as the last of the eight directors, embarking on significant restoration of the landscape throughout, including again the Natural Garden, and defining new areas such as the Sapporo Plaza. As with each predecessor, these two edited the scenery with personal care, guiding the gardens as they grew.

The work to date produced a highly unusual coalescence at the Portland Japanese Garden: it brought together five different styles of gardening into its boundaries. Most locations in Japan rarely exhibit more than one. Part of this had to do with the Garden's mission to demonstrate the riches of its originating culture, but much of this was an extension of Professor Tono's broad ideas. The original 5.5 acres therefore carry a unique mixture of type, character, atmosphere, and detail—a density of art and history played out in scenic terms.

42

The Garden is also special for its backdrop of Pacific Northwest conifers. These towering giants consist of firs, cedars, cypress, and pines. Similar genera can be found in Japan, but the outsized scale, vast abstraction, and bowl-like embrace of vertical lines are specific to the locale. The contrast between low and varied gardens and tall trunks is stark. The trees also frame elevated views of Mount Hood—Oregon's analog to Mount Fuji—vertical slices of *shakkei*, or scenery "borrowed" from more distant vistas, cinematic snippets anchoring the garden to its place. The juxtaposition is possible *only* here, and nowhere else.

Unlikely adjacencies and site characteristics meant that none of this would or could have resembled much older gardens in Japan. And yet, it was just as "Japanese" as those examples, given that Professor Tono's guidance were predicated on essences. Neither the initial Garden Committee nor Tono and the garden directors were preoccupied with verbatim re-creation of Japanese landscape, which would have been impossible. During his first visit, Kengo Kuma remarked with surprise that the Portland Japanese Garden was completely Japanese but had no direct comparison in Japan. Authenticity was not a superficial copy-paste task, but a search for the fundamentals of Japanese landscape design, translated into the local context. The mission was to reveal principles without obligation to presumed appearances.

Described differently, the Portland Japanese Garden marked itself not as a static museum piece but a dynamic, immersive experience. This revelation liberates the Japanese garden from its increasingly museum-like role in Japan, allowing it to be a place of interactive study, and transposes visitor activity from observation to engagement.

The upper pond in the Strolling Pond Garden with the Moon Bridge in the background. Photo: Roman Johnston

Three pivotal individuals committed this shift in practice. The first is Stephen D. Bloom, the current Chief Executive Officer, who with fund-raising aptitude would lead the charge for the Garden's new chapter of growth. He traveled to Japan to understand the potentials of the Garden's circumstances, listening for opportunities in building new connections to the culture. With much needed charisma and unwavering dedication, he spearheaded a new broader vision of international presence and cultural exchange. This included the addition of a Curator of Culture, Art, and Education, and upgrading the Garden Director role to that of Garden Curator, both of which enabled the transformation of the Garden from a local tourist highlight into a cultural leader with tremendous international value. Because of these changes, the organization under Bloom's tenure has seen staff expansion from 17 to 108, annual budget increases from $1.2

TANABE WELCOME
CENTER

ENTRY GARDEN

PAVILION GA

UMAMI CAFÉ

JORDAN SCHNITZER
JAPANESE ARTS
LEARNING CENTER

TATEUCHI
COURTYARD

ELLIE M. HILL
BONSAI TERRACE

GARDEN HOUSE

ZAGUNIS CASTLE WALL

SAND AND STONE GARDEN

NATURAL GARDEN

GARDEN

STROLLING
POND GARDEN

TEA GARDEN

Map of the entire Portland Japanese Garden.
Illustration: Jérôme Mireault, colagene.com

million to $13 million, and membership growth from 3,000 to 17,000. Corresponding annual attendance jumped from 120,000 to roughly 450,000—counted since the new Cultural Village opened in March 2017—with a forecast of more than 500,000 for 2019.

These statistics partially rely on the contribution of Diane Durston, the Arlene Schnitzer Curator of Culture, Art, and Education. With 18 years' scholarship in Kyoto and fluent in both Japanese language and customs, Durston is intimately knowledgeable about a wide array of garden-related arts. Japanese gardens were always tied to tea ceremony, bonsai cultivation, flower arrangement, calligraphy, and the like, and Durston's appointment meant that the Portland Japanese Garden could now develop world-class cultural programs with sensitivity and authority. Her team has enlivened the calendar with workshops, lectures, and celebrations of Japanese festivals and holidays, with special ceremonies by delegations from Tsurugaoka Hachimangu in Kamakura, one of Japan's three most important shrines. Her exhibitions have encompassed ceramics by former Prime Minister

The upper part of the Strolling Pond Garden with the Kashintei Tea House in the background. Photo: Michael Drury

Morihiro Hosokawa, sculptures by Isamu Noguchi, Kabuki costumes and regalia from the renowned theatrical company Shochiku, among many others.

All of this is enabled by the work of Sadafumi Uchiyama, the first Garden Curator at the Portland Japanese Garden. His vocation is closest to the landscape itself, but the title signifies a transition away from top-down direction and toward stewardship over an evolving collection of living art. The position requires a quiet ego and willingness to serve the cycles of nature; Uchiyama's persona is well matched. He is a U.S.–trained landscape architect and a third-generation garden designer coming from southern Japan. Uchiyama's humble manner is reticent toward his deep knowledge, but fastidious craftsmanship and sophisticated work speak in his stead. His contribution is radical in that it calls attention not to him but to the gardens. Uchiyama utilizes the power of editing as an alternative mode of design, or even nondesign. Regarding the recent extension within the garden, he commented "that the site already contained the essential elements we needed and so all what had to be done was to 'edit' it in order to achieve our vision." His approach has paradoxically infused the gardens with continued conceptual resilience and elusive spatial flexibility, a perfect potential pairing for an equally sensitive and worthy architect.

In the long term, this triumvirate would also begin to implement an early concept by Uchiyama and Durston, outlining ideas for teaching technical aspects and methodological underpinnings for the endeavors behind the Garden, relying on in-depth workshops for maintenance and craft. It would be a way of sharing thorough knowledge and practical tools to an audience consisting of serious hobbyists, independent professionals, and more established organizations alike. This would be a catalytic program for other gardens, the foundation for a new International Japanese Garden Training Center. The program's concept is *Waza to Kokoro* ("hands and heart"), created by Uchiyama and Durston to combine technique, thought, and deep personal involvement—an enriched means of learning and understanding. A pilot series of classes constituted the earliest manifestation of this pioneering vision in May 2017.

This newest chapter, however, would not be possible without a crucial intermediate one. Together, Bloom, Durston, and Uchiyama set the scene for a more extroverted, engaged world-class garden. They still needed a way to link all of the pieces, by way of a design that could bind the parts into a meaningful experiential synthesis. In December 2010, the Portland Japanese Garden's Board of Trustees voted for that connective piece, in hiring Kengo Kuma and his team to help realize the Portland Japanese Garden's new Cultural Village.

The original ticketing gate of the Garden with the blooming
sakura of the nearby cherry tree in spring time

The Pavilion Gallery in early dusk

of the Flat Garden and its moss-covered Circle
Gourd Islands in raked white gravel, seen from the
a of the Pavilion Gallery

53

Detail of the Flat Garden showing the moss-covered
Gourd Island in the foreground and the Wet Heron
(*Nure Sagi*) Stone Lantern among dense plants and trees
dressed in bright autumn colors in the background

The Wet Heron (*Nure Sagi*) Lantern of the Flat Garden
in spring. Photo: Ray Pfortner

e Garden's one weeping cherry tree, located in the

Garden

wing pages: The maple tree in the Flat Garden in a

st of autumn colors. Photo: Heinz Holzapfel

le tree south of the Pavilion Gallery in autumn

With its lights on, the Pavilion Gallery and its *engawa*
to retire for the evening of an autumn day. Photo:
nz Holzapfel
wing pages: The Flat Garden with the Pavilion Gallery
from beneath the weeping cherry tree in full
om. Photo: Jonathan Ley

The upper pond of the Strolling Pond Garden in
spring showing the green roofs of the Cultural Village
"disappearing" in the lush greenery

right: Detail of the upper pond in the Strolling Pond
Garden with the small water fall in early autumn

The Moon Bridge in the Strolling Pond Garden
showing also the green roofs of the Cultural Village in
the background as integral parts of the scenery

The celebrated Japanese Laceleaf Maple Tree within
the Strolling Pond Garden in autumn colors. Photo:
David M. Cobb

The frequently photographed Japanese Laceleaf Maple
Tree along the way to the Tea Garden

celebrated Japanese Laceleaf Maple Tree barren of
es along the way to the Tea Garden in early spring
 the view of the upper pond in the Strolling Pond
den behind it

71

left: The two-legged (*Kotoji*) Stone Lantern (a copy of the one which appears in Kenroku-en of Kanazawa; see p.23) along the small stream in the lower Strolling Pond Garden. Photo: Jonathan Ley

following pages: The Heavenly Falls with the stone "Snow-viewing Lantern" (*yukimi-doro*) in the lower pond of the Strolling Garden. Photo: Kenneth Offield

The Zig-Zag (*Yatsuhashi*) Bridge in the lower Strolling
Pond Garden with Japanese irises in early Summer.
Photo: Ray Pfortner

e Zig-Zag (*Yatsuhashi*) Bridge in the lower Strolling
d Garden in mid summer. Photo: Don Schwartz

wing pages: The eighteen-foot-high tiered granite
oda Lantern (*goju-no-to*), donated by Sapporo City
o called the Sapporo Pagoda Lantern), seen with a
ning-red maple tree in the foreground during an
umn evening. Photo: Roman Johnston

Approaching the Kashintei Tea House (*chashitsu*) in its garden. Photo: Tyler Quinn

right: Stepping stones on the way to the south gate of the Tea Garden (*roji*) and Kashintei Tea House
following pages: Toward the east gate of Kashintei Tea House (*chashitsu*). Photo: Tyler Quinn

...rior of the Kashintei Tea House (*chashitsu*) showing
...aised, tatami-covered floors and the decorative
...e (tokonoma) with a scroll of black ink painting
...s back wall

...Near the Kashintei Tea House. Photo: Tyler Quinn

A scene of the Natural Garden. Photo: Dina Avila

orama of the hillside leading into the Natural Garden

ne-paved path with wood handrails in the
tural Garden

Stairway in the Natural Garden in early morning
nmer mist. Photo: Jack Jakobsen
owing pages: Sceneries with Saka's Pond in the
tural Garden. Photo (at left): Bruce Foster

Remote view of the Sand and Stone Garden (*kare-sansui*)
with its eight rocks, seen from above, from the edge of
the Flat Garden south of the Pavilion Gallery. Photo:
Roman Johnston

se-up of the Sand and Stone Garden showing a
up of rocks in carefully raked white gravel against
backdrop of the garden wall whose tiles on top were
dmade in Japan

Monzenmachi—The Cultural Village and Its Architecture

Instead of one heroic shape, we wanted to achieve harmony with the garden. —Kengo Kuma

Since its 1967 opening, the exceptionally well-conceived and attractive Portland Japanese Garden has seen its popularity steadily growing, and so, the only existing Pavilion Gallery, built in 1980, became eventually inadequate. It was then up to Stephen D. Bloom, the Chief Executive Officer since 2005, to spearhead an initiative to expand the Garden with new facilities and new programs. In 2007 the Board of Trustees accepted the proposal, and this was followed by years of intensive fund-raising. The first result was the acquisition of 3.4 additional acres adjacent to the existing 9.1-acre garden to accommodate the new development. Then in 2010, after a careful selection process, Kengo Kuma & Associates was awarded the commission for the design, which effectively launched the realization of Kuma's first public project in North America. Ground breaking took place on August 31, 2015, and the new $37 million Cultural Village opened to the public 50 years after the creation of the Garden, on April 2, 2017. The ground breaking, as well as the opening events, was conducted according to Japanese customs by Chief Priest Shigeho Yoshida from the Tsurugaoka Hachimangu Shinto shrine in Kamakura, who, invited from Japan, blessed first the site and then the completed buildings in elaborate ceremonies.

The requirements for an up-to-date visitors and education center with the commitment to more effective cultivation of Japanese garden design and maintenance as well as to greater promotion of other aspects of Japanese culture in the United States and even beyond, called for several new facilities. Among these were a classroom, a workshop, a garden maintenance and teaching studio, a library, a gift shop, a gallery, an events' space, a café, administrative offices, service spaces, and a new place for ticketing. The Garden is nestled in Washington Park among the city's western rolling hills and is surrounded by the woodlands of magnificent Douglas firs, Big Leaf

The Entry Garden with the illuminated Umami Café seen on top of the hill among the tall firs and cedar trees shrouded in early morning autumn fog

maples, and western red cedars. The serenely resplendent setting of the Garden, known to be the most impressive and authentic one outside Japan, gave considerable challenge to the designers. The obvious task was to fit a relatively large program into an architectural project so that it would not only not harm or diminish the majestic and tranquil beauty of the Garden but also complement and perhaps even enhance it.

From the very beginning of the work, it became clear that, in order not to end up with a large and overwhelming structure, the program had to be arranged in several low-profile buildings. Thus, it was divided into four parts each with related activities, which came to be the Jordan Schnitzer Japanese Arts Learning Center, the Garden House, the Umami Café by Ajinomoto, and a new Ticketing Pavilion, known as the Tanabe Welcome Center. Another important consideration was the siting of the four buildings on the hilly terrain. Previously, visitors purchased their tickets up at the old wood gate, which still marks the actual entrance to the Garden proper. However, the decision was made that while the first three buildings, forming in effect the

Aerial view of the Cultural Village.
Photo: Bruce Forster

Cultural Village, would be clustered in the area next to the Garden at the top of the hill, the Welcome Center with the ticketing office would be placed next to Kingston Avenue at the bottom of the hill. This decision became a significant one, since it also gave a chance for the much-needed redevelopment of the Kingston Avenue area around the pavilion to improve the arrival experience to the Garden and its new facilities.

Thus, at the north side of the new Welcome Center Kuma's office redesigned and extended the parking lot, adding also a more proper boarding area for the shuttle bus that visitors can take up to the Garden. A more important addition here, however, is the terraced water garden on the south side of the Welcome Center. With cascading water flowing into several shallow pools, evocative of the terraced rice paddies (*tanada*) in Japan, this addition, forming a part of the new Entry Garden around, makes an altogether stunningly beautiful introduction to the Garden and the Cultural Village above. Floating over the largest pool, a stone-paved walkway provides another access to the Welcome Center. Here, the views and sounds of the water herald the experience that awaits visitors in the Garden. The Welcome Center with extensive overhanging canopies on each side, works as a gate as well. Passing through under its glass-covered skylight, which accentuates it, one encounters the water garden again before turning on to the elaborate pedestrian path to begin the journey up the hill.

This skillfully choreographed path marks another highlight of the new developments. Although most of the ascending and winding route had already been in place, the section between the Welcome Center and the Antique Gate, donated to the Garden from Japan by the Japan Ancestral Society in 1967, is newly built. This stone-paved, zigzagging walkway that includes stairs and a small bridge also of stone, runs through a landscaped area which forms another part of the Entry Garden. This landscaped area, like several others in the whole compound, was created by Garden Curator Sadafumi Uchiyama. It features plenty of stones in the form of large rocks, in addition to a palette of plants. Leaving behind the Entry Garden, one can follow the meandering path which, beyond the Antique Gate becomes steeper and the walk gradually quieter and more contemplative. Along the way one can catch the first fleeting glimpses of the Cultural Village high up on the hill among the towering trees. The occasional flashes of the buildings, variously filtered through the foliage, increase the anticipation of what awaits the visitor above.

The peaceful drama of this approach is the result of both the breathtaking topography of the wooded terrain and the designers' inspired response to it. The experience of the uphill journey is enhanced by Uchiyama's rich

replanting of the hillside and the architect's perceptive sequencing of the approach and arrival. As one gets closer to the Cultural Village, the sharply cantilevered structure of the Umami Café, floating effortlessly above the steep terrain, is the first building to come into view from the path below. Here a large crevice called for the construction of a pedestrian bridge, which Kuma's team designed as an elegant, stone-paved steel structure with glass balustrades, known as Sheila's Bridge. Although a bridge is always

95

a passage, this time it is also a prominent place to pause. Here, on one side, visitors can marvel at the sights of the dramatic yet graceful architecture and the verdant swale with a Japanese cherry tree at its top; on the other side, they can look back at the majestic wooded landscape below and the just-traveled path. The final steps, an open stairway next to the Umami Café takes one up to the Tateuchi Courtyard, the place of "arrival." Altogether, the much rewarding journey here is not unlike the ones experienced when approaching Shinto shrines or Buddhist temples in Japan.

The opening ceremony of the Cultural Village was conducted according to Japanese Shinto customs by Chief Priest Shigeo Yoshida from the Tsurugaoka Hachimangu Shinto shrine in Kamakura on the rainy day of April 2, 2017. Photo: Tyler Quinn

Stepping onto the black granite-paved courtyard, visitors are welcomed by the embrace of the surrounding buildings. Two of them recede in zigzag fashion toward the west, where the tapered space between them with the adjacent shuttle bus drop-off area at the back signals another entrance to the Village. The "flying geese" arrangement of the Learning Center and the Garden House reflects the typical layout of Japanese buildings, as seen, for example, at the famous seventeenth-century Katsura Imperial Villa in Kyoto, which Kuma knows well and much admires. Yet, in the architecture of the

Village, there are several other clues that betray Japanese sensibility. In fact, the design of the Village itself is an unmistakable allusion to the numerous traditional *monzen-machi,* the small settlements built in front of the gate of a temple or shrine. According to Uchiyama, the setting here is also reminiscent of the "quintessential border zone between mountain foothills and arable land (*satoyama*) in Japan, where everyday life coexists with nature, providing the perfect location for the new Cultural Village."

The Umami Café at the east end, next to the main entry, is only a single-story structure, but the others are two-story buildings. Here, the second stories step back on each side from the first ones, a common feature in many temples as well as urban residences (*machiya*) in Japan. Moreover, extensive hipped roofs cover all three buildings; the Café is capped by one, while the others by two, in double-tiered arrangement. On the upper ones, green local sedums have been planted, providing a highly innovative solution: this, on the one hand, helps the buildings blend into the verdant surroundings and, on the other hand, channels rainwater into the drainage

Tea ceremony (*chado*) demonstration in the Cathy Rudd Cultural Corner of the Jordan Schnitzer Japanese Arts Learning Center of the Cultural Village. Photo: Jonathan Ley

system. Portland has a rather wet climate, similar to Japan's; just as in Japan, the deep eaves serve to protect one from heavy rain, while creating a distinctive zone beneath, a quasi *engawa,* between inside and outside, all around the buildings.

All these buildings are designed with steel-frame structures wherein most other materials are glass and, more so, wood. The Umami Café, which overlooks the steep slope, the Antique Gate, and the Entry Garden, way below, is wrapped in floor-to-ceiling sliding glass walls on three of its sides. These walls can be opened to generous balconies that provide additional seating in good weather, some in the shade of the blooming sakura of the nearby cherry tree during the proper season. Most of the interiors, designed also by Kuma's office, are finished with natural cedar. In the Café, however, one large triangular segment of the ceiling is a skylight, whose glass surface is covered with ordinary Tyvek sheets that filter light in a manner similar to Japanese *washi* paper. This marvelous small building, akin to a proverbial tree house, takes its cue not only from the café in the garden of Kuma's 2009 Nezu Museum in Tokyo but also, in both cases, from the main structure of the seventeenth-century Kiyomizu Temple in Kyoto, which was constructed high over the steep hillside of Higashiyama.

The Garden House features service areas and the horticultural or garden maintenance workshop, which doubles as a garage on its ground floor, as well as the Robert W. Franz Garden Curator's office and staff rooms for resident gardeners on the upper one. On the other side, the

Learning Center houses the event space, called the Jane Stimson Miller "Living Room," the Tanabe Gallery, the gift shop, the multipurpose Yanai classroom, the Lixil Mechanical, Electrical, and Plumbing compound, and other services on the first floor, and the Vollum Library, the Franklin D. Piacentini Executive office and terrace, and other administrative offices on the second. Both buildings are carefully integrated into the sloping hills behind; thus they have on-grade exits on the second levels and outside stairs from them as well. In case of the Learning Center, this takes the form of a bonsai terrace, named the Jubitz Oregon Terrace, a surprising small and quiet, elevated garden. These buildings have large fixed wood panels as well as fixed and sliding glass walls as parts of their ground-floor facades, whereas on the second floors there are continuous ribbon-windows. However, at the Learning Center, similar to the Welcome Center, both the fixed and the movable glass walls are outfitted with vertical wood slats, another hallmark of Kuma's architecture, here with variable density, echoing the random setting of the surrounding trees. They work as a visual filter that provides some privacy to the inside activities.

The Village plaza, called Tateuchi Courtyard, of the Cultural Village seen from its south-east corner in early morning autumn fog

Such arrangement is particularly important in case of the multipurpose Living Room, which is in many ways the most impressive indoor public space in the Cultural Village. First of all, here all the glass wall-panels, which wrap around the corner, can be opened entirely, thus connecting the interior with the exterior directly. This connection is intensified by the clever elimination—or, more precisely, the repositioning—of the steel corner post. As a result of all these, the Learning Center, perhaps more than the other two buildings, renders the partially enclosed courtyard also as an intimate "indoor" place. At the same time, this corner, named the Cathy Rudd Cultural Corner, features an elevated four-and-a-half-tatami-mat platform, which serves partly as a place for tea-ceremony demonstrations and other events, partly to display various pieces of Japanese art, all of which can be seen from both the inside and, when the walls are open, the outside. Furthermore, the interior of this double-story Living Room is enveloped in vibrant layers of densely spaced wood slats, which endow its space with the captivating quality of uplifting lightness. This quality, though, is as much the result of the uniquely designed, wide, wood grand stairway. Here every other step is deeper and extended all the way to the partition of vertical slats and functions as tiered seating, from where visitors can view the events taking place on either the tatami platform or the adjacent open place serving also as an ad hoc stage. The Living Room connects directly to the space of the adjacent small art gallery elevating the totality of the experience even further.

following pages: Hand-drawn sketch of the Cultural Village by Kengo Kuma

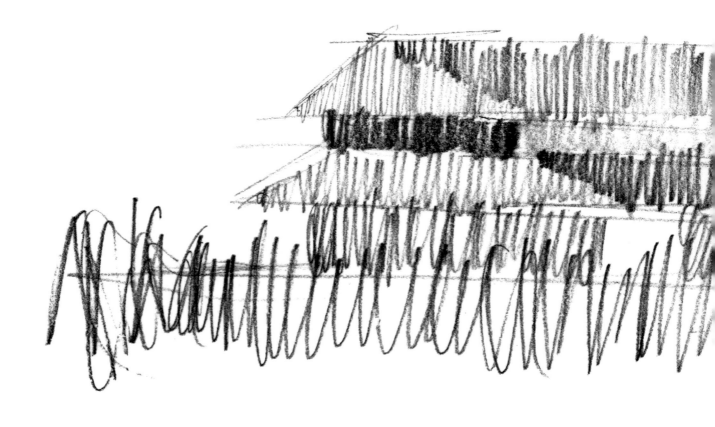

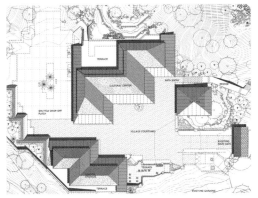

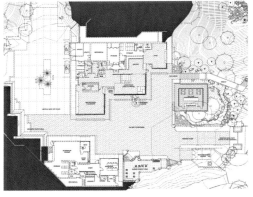

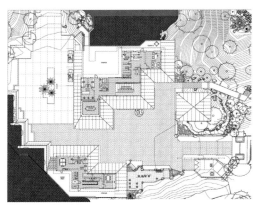

Site plan, and first and second floor plans of the Cultural Village. Drawings: courtesy of Kengo Kuma & Associates (KKAA)

The Courtyard is a supremely important part of the design, for as an intimate public place it holds together the Cultural Village as a distinct assemblage, and so, the Courtyard emerges as its heart and soul. Perhaps it is not farfetched to compare it to the empty courtyards of neighborhood Shinto shrine compounds where, owing to the historical lack of urban plazas in Japan, the community could gather for various activities including festivals. The Courtyard of the Cultural Village works in similar way; here the festive Shinto ceremonies of both the ground breaking and the opening of the new project were held, and it is here where numerous performances, such as kabuki, are scheduled. This Courtyard, like some dry or rock garden, could also stand for that "void" in Japanese understanding of place-time continuity, to which everything relates and from which everything emanates. Here, by way of its presence and sensitively calibrated scale, the Courtyard activates the spaces of its surrounding buildings into which it variably penetrates.

Nevertheless, the boundaries of this Courtyard are not limited to only the three buildings alone; at the west side, there was a need to retain the steep slope of the hill to prevent landslides. Instead of the usual (and certainly not the most attractive) reinforced concrete retaining wall, Uchiyama recommended using a type of medieval stone structure and technique that created the massive ramparts of feudal castles in Japan. Kuma's wall here, called the Zagunis Castle Wall, built with regional Baker Blue granite boulders, continues the zigzag formation of the buildings in a highly graceful manner. This exceptional wall here is actually the first such new construction of this ancient type of wall after about four hundred years and, interestingly, not in Japan but in the United States, representing, like so many parts and aspects of the new Cultural Village, a true "cultural crossing" between the two countries.

Other parts of the Courtyard's edge, however, remain much softer; Uchiyama was on board again with two very special small gardens, the *tsubo niwa* next to the Learning Center, and the Ellie M. Hill Bonsai Terrace, east of the Garden House. The first, featuring the essential elements of Japanese gardens: stone, plants, and water in a very small area, is an artistic accent that is embraced by the Living Room, when its glass wall-panels are open. At the same time, the Bonsai Terrace with some centuries-old small, potted trees, is part of the long border that the Courtyard shares on its south side with the existing Japanese

Garden unfolding below. Looking back toward the new Cultural Village from the winding paths of the Garden, visitors can observe the receding views of the architecture revealing only its green roofs for a while, before they, too, give way to the wonderfully rewarding experience of the Japanese Garden itself. Yet, at the end, one is left with the feeling that this experience is greatly intensified by the masterful addition of the Cultural Village and that the two, indeed in a symbiotic relationship, mutually complement and enhance each other.

As Randy Gragg, director of the University of Oregon's John Yeon Center for Architectural Studies and the Landscapes and former architecture critic for The Oregonian stated: "The Portland Japanese Garden's addition by Kengo Kuma and his team is a watershed moment for the city: not just a masterful match of building design to site and purpose, but a reach, culturally, beyond our usual modest ambitions." Then the Portland Japanese Garden's own Arlene Schnitzer Curator of Culture, Art, and Education Diane Durston commented this way: "With expansive views, natural materials, a humble footprint, and spaces that respond to the changing seasons, Kuma has provided us with an architecture of art and crafts that places expressions of the human spirit within the humbling embrace of nature in our Garden. This place is a physical manifestation of *kokoro*, the Japanese belief in the harmony of heart and mind, man and nature, as the single most important principle of a balanced life."

right: The Tanabe Welcome Center and Ticketing
Pavilion seen together with the terraced water garden,
the shallow reflecting pool, and the approaching
passage "floating" above it
following pages, left: Entrance through the Welcome Center
following pages, right: Detail of the terraced water garden
also showing in the background a small retaining
wall rendered as the stone ramparts of medieval
Japanese castles

Detail of the Welcome Center with the densely spaced
wooden slats as its south facade

Leaving behind the Cultural Village at the top of the hill, visitors exit back through the Antique Gate

Climbing most of the steep pedestrian path on the
hillside, buildings of the Cultural Village emerge
more prominently

right: Remote view of the Cultural Village enveloped in the deep green foliage of tall Douglas firs and western red cedars during late summer. Photo: James Florio
following pages, left: The buildings of the Cultural Village viewed from the elegant structure of Sheila's Bridge
following pages, right: The Umami Café and the nearby cherry tree in full bloom seen from the vantage point of visitors as they pose on Sheila's Bridge

The scenery welcoming the visitors after scaling the
final stairs and arriving at the east entry-point to the
Cultural Village

...receding and tapered space of the Tateuchi
...rtyard, defined by the zigzagging volumes of the
...ing Garden House on the left and the Learning
...er on the right; viewed from under the eaves of
...Umami Café

The Umami Café with the east entry point to its left
seen from under the eaves of the Learning Center in
early morning autumn fog

Through the open sliding glass walls, the interior of the Umami Café connects directly to its surrounding veranda under the deep eaves of the roof, while the Learning Center appears in the background.

The Umami Café's dramatically cantilevered structure
at the east end of Tateuchi Courtyard hovers above the
sharply sloping terrain and the approaching stairway.

Interior of the Umami Café with its cedar-paneled ceiling and triangular skylight, wrapped around in story-high sliding glass walls providing excellent views of the surrounding wooded landscape

Preparing tea in the Umami Café. Photo: Esther Huyn

128

The Tateuchi Courtyard viewed from under the eaves
of the Garden House

The stone-paved path lined with bamboo, leading
from the Tateuchi Courtyard to the Old Main Gate
(not visible here) of the Garden

The Tateuchi Courtyard and the Learning Center seen
from an upper-floor office window of the Garden House

GIFT SHOP

The Learning Center with its sliding glass walls
and vertical wood slats open reveals the elevated,
tatami-covered platform of the Cultural Corner and
the illuminated interior of the Jane Stimson Miller
"Living Room." With its lights on, the interior of the
Gift Shop (to the right) can be seen through the glass
walls and vertical slats.

With the repositioned corner post of the structural
frame, the space of the Cultural Corner as well as
the Living Room behind can merge without any
obstruction with the outside courtyard and the small
Tsubo Niwa (on the left), when the sliding walls are open
on both sides.

The interior of the Living Room showing the Cultural Corner with all glass walls around closed. Views of the outside are generous yet filtered through the vertical wood slats, here variably spaced to respond to the similarly located trees around. The ceilings in this event space are finished in bamboo panels whose natural color renders everything in warm glow. Photo: James Florio

140

In the Living Room, the most dynamic element is the major stairway. Its wood steps have been designed so that every other one with double width and height would extend all to way to the adjacent wall of dense vertical slats to provide tiered seating for visitors viewing the occasional performances in this event space. Photo: James Florio

The Living Room looking past the main stairway toward the entrance and the small Tanabe Art Gallery on the left. Photo James Florio

144

Looking back from the top of the stairway on the
second floor reveals the passage to the Franklin D.
Piacentini Executive Office and the cavernous double-
height space of the Living Room. Photo: James Florio

The Vollum Library on the second floor of the
Learning Center features shelves for essential books on
Japanese Gardening and a large, unusually attractive
wood table designed by George Nakashima.

right: The second floor of the Learning Center includes a rooftop garden, called the Jubitz Oregon Terrace, over part of the first floor

following pages: Another, and equally innovative, new addition to the existing garden is the Ellie M. Hill Bonsai Terrace east of the Garden House. This "garden" features numerous rare, centuries-old potted trees, which are on loan to Portland Japanese Garden from regional artists and displayed under proper weather conditions and occasions.

Craftsmanship in the Design and Construction of the Cultural Village

Material is not a finish—Kengo Kuma

Craft is not merely detail. It is also materiality, technique, and the experts fusing those together. From the outset, the Portland Japanese Garden's clearly aimed wholehearted effort has been imbued with the very highest standards. This pervaded everything from ambitious vision to design team selection, all the way to attention to material joinery. The pursuit of a well-made project was a trend established in the decades preceding the new Cultural Village, reinforced by the methodical work of Garden Curator Sadafumi Uchiyama and his team and now carried forward by Kengo Kuma & Associates. Craft as a concept of deliberate decision defined the spirit of the project from start to finish. Quality was to be present in the approach as well as in the final artifact.

The painstakingly designed *Tsubo Niwa*, featuring all the essential components of a Japanese garden: plant, rock, and water in a tiny and unenclosed plot, adds an artistic counterpoint to both the Tateuchi Courtyard and the entire garden precinct

Immediately evident are the rich natural materials throughout the project—not only in the architecture but also in the landscape. Eaves and screens of Oregon-native Alaskan yellow cedar mingle with strategically positioned living Douglas firs and Japanese maple, while textured paving and walls of local granite ground a vast selection of Oregonian flora in the new gardens. Specific to place and project alike, the combinations compose a seamless, living, breathing palette.

The new buildings encompass a limited, muted array as a way to keep the focus on the lushness of the surrounding gardens and the entirety of the visitor journey. Three principal materials define the exteriors: vegetated upper roofs, patterned metal lower roofs, and the aforementioned Alaskan yellow cedar. The extensive glass is experientially immaterial, allowing in broad framed views of the gardens and dissolving building edges by cloaking them in reflections. The architecture thus defers to the landscape even through its materials.

left: Detail of the densely spaced vertical wood slats on the Living Room back wall

The interiors maintain uncluttered cohesion with a balance of Port Orford cedar and simple white-painted walls. Secondary materials reward closer viewing: bamboo (the ceilings at the Jordan Schnitzer Japanese Arts Learning Center, the Cultural Village's largest building), lightened white oak (the upper floors), dark granite, and hand-whitewashed oriented-strand-board panels (the ceilings in the Garden House). Kuma intentionally selected compatible colors and textures to unify the atmosphere within.

Local provenance largely dictated final selection, but materials were chosen also owing to their capacity to span culture and time-tested techniques. A major goal of the Portland Japanese Garden has been to use the new project as an active teaching tool, demonstrative of long-standing Japanese traditions with area methods and expertise. Craft and technique serve as a visual, tangible manifestation of a larger cultural dialog. Not immediately obvious without closer examination, select techniques fall into two basic categories: traditional methods deployed with modern abstraction, and modern technologies with traditional expression.

above top: Several handheld tools used by Japan-trained American craftsman Dale Brotherton, for executing meticulous detail in wood. Photo: Bruce Forster
above bottom: Brotherton hand-planes all of the Port Orford Cedar for the interior screens, yielding silken smooth surfaces, paper-thin leftovers, and an intoxicating wooden fragrance. Photo: Bruce Forster
right: The warmth of Alaskan Yellow Cedar pervades the building exteriors, as vertical louver screens emulating the pattern of nearby old-growth trees, and as a tongue-and-groove surfaces beneath the roof eaves.

154

The first category—traditional methods deployed with modern abstraction—encompasses materials worked by traditional Japanese techniques and subtly updated by American implementation: the Port Orford cedar, the chestnut wood main doors, and the granite castle walls.

Port Orford cedar is revered for its intoxicating fragrance as well as its durability and its gracefully soft silver-gray ageing. These characteristics of Port Orford cedar, which resembles hinoki, or Japanese cypress, emerge in two key architectural elements: the wood screen in the main building's Jane Stimson Miller Living Room, and the levitating lapped plank ceiling at the Umami Café by Ajinomoto.

For the Living Room screen, Kuma chose to show the cedar purely as material and technique, distilling the traditional *kōshi* screen to a barcode of delicate vertical slats. For such refinement, Kuma's team worked closely with Japan-trained, Seattle-based woodworker Dale Brotherton, who retains a nuanced appreciation for both wood and Japanese woodworking principles. Silken smooth louvers exude machinelike precision throughout, spaced to demanding tolerances—executed *entirely* by hand. Small plugs of the cedar conceal all mechanical fasteners. Even the painstakingly consistent one-sixteenth-inch corner bevels were completed with traditional hand planes. Nothing was sanded.

The same is true for the Café's ceiling, featuring *yamato-bari,* a Japanese detail for overlapping wood pieces. Compared to the screen, the surfaces are

broader and the demand for flawlessness much higher. Brotherton applied the same level of attention to the soft luster and tapered edges of the cedar boards. He also spliced linear LED lighting into the one-inch gaps between planks, integrating the components so as to remain as invisible as possible. Though difficult to achieve, the result bears understated visual luxury—elevating Port Orford cedar from coveted species to Japanese sublimity.

While American-worked American wood provided the centerpieces for the interiors, Japanese-worked Japanese wood became a symbolic counterbalance at the main doors. Kuma invited revered Kyoto craftsman Yoshiaki Nakamura to work on the project, based on his leading mastery of a dwindling labor-intensive technique called *naguri*. This requires a flat-headed adze called a *chōna*; its use had long allowed traditional Japanese craftsmen to

approximate flat surfaces with simple means. The woodworker loads body weight onto narrow pieces to keep the wood in place, swinging the razor-sharp *chōna* downward to remove small, precisely spaced chips. For the project this was repeated with control over nearly 2,500 linear feet of *kuri*, or Japanese chestnut. This tough species ages beautifully with touch, showing uniformly flecked character in the grain.

Nakamura could not travel to Portland for installation, adding logistical challenge to the large, complex pivoting doors. Normally his workshop fabricates the entire door, but instead Hoffman Construction Company had to create the steel and wood frames in Portland, receiving the *naguri* pieces from Japan. They relied on Kuma's project architect and Uchiyama to interpret detailed diagrammed instructions, deploying their own carpenters for the final assembly. Overseas coordination nevertheless yielded two impressive double-sided front doors, one each for the Learning Center and the Garden House.

157

above top: The primary tools of choice for master stonemason Suminori Awata keep to an impossibly limited array of chisel and mallet. Photo: Bruce Forster
above bottom: A zigzagging extension of both architecture and landscape, the Castle Wall welcomes visitors arriving at the upper west entry.
left: The Zagunis Castle Wall features a generations-old Japanese dry technique that relies on gravity alone to strengthen the fit of the stone, at once highly precise and improvisational

The final tour de force of Japanese technique lies with the Zagunis Castle Wall. Originally conceived by Kuma and Uchiyama as a continuation of the zigzagging architecture into the landscape, this wall forms the backdrop to the Cultural Village's central courtyard and keeps the surrounding terrain at bay. Yet the design team had no way to realize such a formidable gesture without authentic expertise.

Uchiyama introduced Suminori Awata, a 15th-generation stonemason from one of the few families maintaining existing castle walls throughout Japan. These walls adhere to the *Ano-zumi* tradition of dry assembly, using only gravity and fit, without fastenings or mortar. Gaps allow the wedges to settle, with inward action of the stone's weight locking pieces together and adding strength over time. Nevertheless, with feudal society now centuries past, even Awata's predecessors rarely saw new castle construction. The one for the Portland Japanese Garden would be the opportunity of his lifetime.

Awata worked only with veteran Californian stonemasons Matt Driscoll and Kyle Schlagenhauf, adding technical support from Oregonian Ed

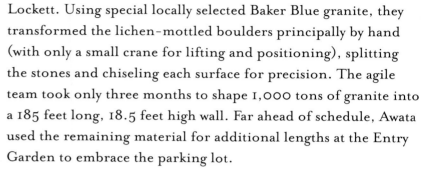

Lockett. Using special locally selected Baker Blue granite, they transformed the lichen-mottled boulders principally by hand (with only a small crane for lifting and positioning), splitting the stones and chiseling each surface for precision. The agile team took only three months to shape 1,000 tons of granite into a 185 feet long, 18.5 feet high wall. Far ahead of schedule, Awata used the remaining material for additional lengths at the Entry Garden to embrace the parking lot.

The test-bed for the vegetated panels lie in wait at Komatsu Seiren, eventually the precursor to those planted on site in advance of installation at the Cultural Village. Photo: Bruce Forster

The stone faces bear the stylistic differences between the three. Awata tended to the cornerstones with disciplined and consistent strikes, while Driscoll's and Schlagenhauf's marks exude more varied energy in the bodies of the walls. The combination is a subtle cultural conversation in masonry— the only common language between the Japanese and the Americans. This is the first castle wall in the world to combine both Japanese and American techniques.

158

The second set of techniques uses new materials to achieve traditional expression. Modern elements risk detraction from the time-honored gardens, but Kuma avoids incompatible aesthetics—contemporary materials always serve older motifs, standing in where conventional materials prove insufficient. The reversal is used in selected instances only, with an eye on the totality of the architecture and the landscape surrounding it. Technology must be discreet.

Directional installation of the pre-planted panels correspond to the orientation of available light. Photo: Bruce Forster

The vegetated roofs are the most visually present, if not an overtly new, technology. The innovation is that they use no soil at all, compared to the typical minimum of 4 inches of soil for planting beds. Instead, local sedum species embed roots directly into three-fourths of an inch of thin microporous ceramic panels called GreenBiz—a by-product of textile company Komatsu Seiren's dyeing processes. The panels fulfilled three demands. Aesthetically, they allowed Kuma's team to express the edges as thin lines, reducing the perceived weight of the roof. For the vegetation, panel porosity balanced both rainwater shed and modest water retention, critical to its growth. Finally, the plantings helped the buildings to recede into their towering arboreal context, fusing architecture and nature.

right: With time, the vegetation is intended to overgrow the edges of the roof, softening the architecture into its surroundings, and making visible the path of water from sky to plant, roof, and ground—a legible story that avoids conventional gutters and drains. Photo: James Florio

Metal roofs in crisp plates lie lower in the architecture, their modern

silhouette reminiscent of older Japanese villages. These aluminum surfaces indicate hand-burnished gray textures, but application by hand was simply cost-prohibitive. Instead, Kuma's team worked with Japanese company DNP and their American partner Pure + FreeForm to scan a hand-brushed sample and print it directly on to thin aluminum veneer. This was then adhered to thicker aluminum stock and precisely trimmed to size, yielding faster and more durable results. It was a complex procedure blending humanmade patterns and advanced technologies, and this ambiguity prevented the aluminum roofs from being out of place.

The Umami Café's skylight is the last example of deceptive appearance, with a translucent triangular swatch drawing the eye upward. Ordinarily *washi*, or Japanese rice paper, appeared in wall partitions but Kuma chose to accent

The ceiling at Umami Café levitates above the space, generously framing the surrounding landscape on three of four sides

left: A minimalist palette with compositional impact, the ceiling at Umami Café choreographs hand-planed Port Orford cedar panels, Japanese rice paper-like Tyvek sheet, and integrated LED lights.

the ceiling instead, to protect the Café's 270-degree panorama. This material in such a space would be atmospherically impressive, but maintenance and condensation make paper too unsuitably delicate for a skylight cover. Kuma's team relied on a substitute that was not only tear- and water-resistant but also texturally almost as fibrous as the paper, identical when backlit. This material, commercially called Tyvek and often seen as mail packaging, is normally used as construction building wrap. It ably filters changing season, weather, and time of day, suffusing the intimate space with soft shifts of light and shadow. This scrim masquerades as *washi*, although the effects of the more robust material remain faithful to its forebear.

If the project were only to be regarded for its tangible and visible aspects, then a significant part of the story of the Cultural Village would remain untold. "Craft" played a far more nuanced role in the case of the Portland Japanese Garden—critically important is that it was action as much as intended result, and mentality as much as finished artifact. The design depended deeply on a crafted *process* to deliver the desired result.

The selection of Kengo Kuma and his team was a significant moment in the Portland Japanese Garden's growth, but it was by no means the end or even the start. Predating them was the hiring of Stephen D. Bloom, Diane Durston, and Sadafumi Uchiyama, charged with the aforementioned vision to push the organization's international prominence. The Garden in turn selected Kengo Kuma & Associates only after lengthy research, involving interviews and visits to architects' offices in Japan, followed by a two-stage design competition. Kuma's team matched their values—holding the existing gardens as the most important aspect of the new design.

Their selection set the pace for similar rigor in choosing the Architect of Record, the Landscape Architect, and the Landscape Architect of Record. All team members were to be the best fit for the assignment. With lengthy discussion and some hesitation (owing to dual client and designer roles, and established tradition before him), Sadafumi Uchiyama joined as the Landscape Architect, representing the next wave of development for the gardens and balancing the equally respectful Kuma. Both the Portland Japanese Garden and Kuma's team selected Hacker Architects as Architect of Record and Walker Macy as Landscape Architect of Record for their collective experience and deep passion for materials and detail—shared affinities among all the designers. Both supporting offices are renowned in their own right, but here graciously recognized Kengo Kuma & Associates' design leadership.

Quality can only emerge from effective communication, and the principal team members were already chosen with this criterion in mind. Clarity depends entirely on media *and* methods—for the design team was spread over geographical, temporal, and cultural distance. As added reinforcement, Kuma's project architect and Uchiyama bridged the linguistic divide at every stage.

Examples of some tools of the kind used by Kyoto master craftsman Yoshiaki Nakamura, again indicating that precision and rich character of wood can emerge from hand techniques. Photo: Bruce Forster

Significantly, the Portland Japanese Garden made two decisions even before the designing began. First, it embarked on a similar and unconventionally early selection process for the General Contractor—the aforementioned Hoffman Construction Company—to monitor costs and engage conversations about assembly and detail, from the start. Second, it established a Special Project Oversight Committee (composed of client representatives, design team members, members from the City of Portland, and respected advisers) to ensure continual focus on quality.

In the background, the design team quickly set out ample means of trading ideas. Kuma's side built dozens of models per phase at multiple scales, along with hundreds of sketches for internal discussion. Regular consultation with Kuma yielded incremental and methodical spatial tests. The best of these were shared with Hacker Architects via online conferencing—a truly minuscule proportion of studies. Later stages saw the architect team work with detailed parallel digital models in both Tokyo and Portland to ensure thorough coordination through construction.

Uchiyama's concepts entered via his own eloquent hand drawings, often resulting from conversations with Kuma, and were reinforced with Walker Macy's technical imagination. Uchiyama was instrumental in selecting materials and positioning stones and plants alike, making sure each finessed angle and orientation attained the "correct" behavior of the materials.

right: Nakamura's hand-worked doors feature chestnut wood pieces shipped from his studio in Japan, using a traditional *adze*. This is the inner surface of the main door at the Learning Center, a tactile celebration of the act of entry.

Since January 2013, weekly team phone calls and online conversations supplemented monthly visits by Kuma's project architect. Kengo Kuma himself visited the site several times yearly despite burgeoning international demand, from early phases through construction. His palpable enthusiasm carried through to thorough checks of life-size mock-ups of details and materials, with teams correcting to his comments.

Central to the execution of the work was Hoffman Construction Company; its expert teams diligently kept stride with the designers' risks and requests, both pushing back with knowledgeable recommendations and listening to new ideas. Theirs was a collaborative attitude similar to that expected in Japan. Internal push and pull reflected a shared goal of delivering relentlessly beautiful work.

The approach was disciplined and organized, but improvisation was just as essential. Weather and misinterpretations forced the team to frequently fine-tune details. New partial-scale models described corrections, with Kuma's project architect relaying photos from Portland to Tokyo for confirmation. Rather than dogged adherence to a fixed design, nimble decisions allowed for reasonable modification to achieve satisfying aesthetics. This flexibility allowed for circumstance-specific responses at every step of the construction—an ultimately precise outcome despite numerous small changes.

Therefore, the instances of the project's craft are not merely static art objects, but dynamic entities that oscillate between traditional technique with modern manifestation, and vice versa, and with multiple invisible processes guiding their combination to reality. Craftsmanship was ultimately not as simple as selecting a material local to Oregon and devising a beautiful detail for it. Instead, the design drew on the best knowledge from Japan and the Pacific Northwest. The result was a transpacific, flexible back-and-forth iterative discussion of surprising cultural exchange, and a cyclical process across generations and geography—manifested in carefully crafted architecture.

left: Closer viewing of the Nakamura's chestnut wood reveals the capacity of the human hand to achieve depth of texture and character in the material, somewhere between impossible consistency, subtle tonal variations, and nearly indiscernible but necessary "error."

Appendix: The Architecture of Kengo Kuma

*I try to listen to the site as carefully as possible . . . because I believe
that a building should become one with its surroundings. . . . It is a
condition in which the building and environment dissolve into one.*
—Kengo Kuma

Kengo Kuma is one of Japan's most prominent and prolific architects;
in addition to his main office in Tokyo, he also runs a much-recognized
international practice with branch offices in Paris, Beijing, and Shanghai.
His many completed projects in Japan as well as abroad encompass an
unusually wide variety in both size and type of architecture, ranging from
the very simple, small structures of Japanese tearooms, to such large, high-
tech, and important complexes as the 2018 V&A Dundee—Scotland's first
design museum and the only Victoria and Albert Museum outside London—
and the New National Stadium for the 2020 Olympic Games in Tokyo.
Linking his works together are a sophisticated simplicity, a restraint in form-
making, a high level of craftsmanship, and, by means of his skillful use of
materials, a heightened sensory, even sensual quality of space and a particular
sense of lightness and warmth, as well as a better response to locality and the
broader environment.

Moreover, Kuma's architecture, in conjunction with his uncommon
penchant for widely different materials, construction technologies, and
sources of inspiration, also reveals his total independence from any
particular, formalized style or fashion. Altogether, they attest to a free-
spirited yet restrained mode of design. He wrote: "I want to produce
architecture freely without feeling constrained by specific techniques or
methods. . . . More than, and prior to defining a style, what I desire is to
create a certain type of place and a certain type of condition that can be
experienced by the human body. Starting out from human sensations,
I want to arrive at an architecture that utilizes everything, from traditional
techniques to the most advanced technology." Although not easily identifiable
with any trend, his impressively variegated work epitomizes one of the most
significant examples in contemporary Japanese architecture.

The GC Prostho Museum and
Research Center, Kasugai, Japan,
2010. The museum's structural system
of wood uses no glue at all.

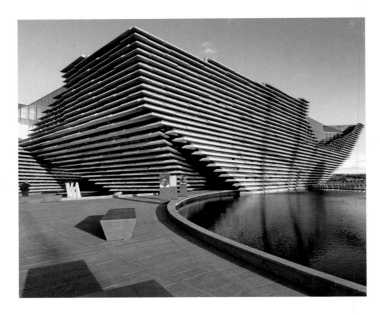

Kuma's goal is to engender the conditions for intimate yet active relationships between humans and their environment or the world that could diminish their prevailing dichotomy. He has set out to do this on the level not only of emotions but also of deep consciousness that necessarily involves existential or ontological concerns. He is convinced that in fostering such a relationship, architecture as a field of connections, and so a catalyst, can play a significant role. However, he also recognizes that architecture can fulfill such a role only if it is removed as much as possible from the realm of objects. A prolific writer with a prodigious knowledge of contemporary society, architectural history, and philosophy, Kuma has written extensively on the subject. In his book *Anti-Object* (2007), he wrote, "[A]n object is a form of material existence distinct from its immediate environment. I do not deny that all buildings . . . are to some extent objects. However, buildings that are deliberately made distinct from their environment are very different from those that attempt to mitigate this isolation, and the difference is perceptible to everyone who experiences them." To lessen this isolation, Kuma has developed specific design strategies.

First, as a critical reaction to the flamboyant, excessively image-driven and too often reckless practices that inflicted both visual and physical harm on the natural and urban environments during the previous bubble economy in Japan, Kuma, after the mid-1990s, began to steer his architecture toward a special genre of minimalism. In certain conditions this meant to make his buildings disappear by burying them under the ground. In case of the Kiro-san Observatory of 1994 on the peak of a picturesque mountain, he carved the structure into the land rather than violate the scenic landscape of the small Japanese island with an object. Although earth has remained an important material for him, other means have also emerged in his explorations. He realized that "breaking down" some components of his buildings into *particles* could also be an effective way to render his architecture less object-like. Increasingly, various louver systems, densely spaced slats, and many kinds of delicate screens became instrumental in configuring his architecture. Yet, while the filigrees of "woven" elements endow his buildings with a palpable or hallucinatory vibrancy, their overall forms are kept invariably as simple as possible.

The appeal of this mode of design he calls "particlization" is brought about by the special application of the widest range of materials. In addition to the usual steel, glass, aluminum, and fiber-glass-reinforced plastic, the ones he uses most willingly are natural ones: water, earth, stone, clay, tiles, various fabrics, plants, dry reeds, paper, bamboo, thatch, and especially wood. In this regard, it is important that, as part of his efforts to advance

clockwise, from top left:
V&A Museum Dundee, Scotland, 2018; Water / Cherry Villa, Ito, Japan, 2013; Suteki House, Happy Valley, OR, USA, 2017; Nezu Art Museum, Tokyo, 2009; Nagasaki Prefectural Museum of Art, 2005; Jeju Ball, Lotte Art Village, Jeju Island, Korea, 2013

the architectural culture of a given place or region, he seeks out and uses *local* materials. Such intentions are even more significant when the site of his project is still occupied with an existing and salvageable building. Rather than tearing it down, Kuma is eager to reuse as much as possible of the old structure and its materials while adapting the new design accordingly. Employing materials in his "particular" way, he is able not only to render the boundaries of his buildings sensibly layered, soft, and ambiguous, but also to attenuate their size and volume and, so, their dominating presence even when creating larger buildings. His works tend to seem fragile and evanescent; they appear to gently recede into their surrounding natural or urban landscape. Kuma does not strive for striking monumentality or for the highly idiosyncratic, if not bizarre, kind of architecture so common today.

Architect and architecture critic Juhani Pallasmaa put it this way: "Kengo Kuma is an architect who aims at a distinct quietness, a disciplined understatement in his architectural expression, and the disengagement of his architect's persona," to which it should be added that such outward anonymity is by no means a sign of artistic conservativism. This is proven as much by many of his modern, even futuristic design renditions as by his own words: "My wish is to use today's advanced technologies in combination with local natural materials [and] technique[s;] . . . in other words, in my work I attempt to bridge the traditional and the innovative, as well as the local and the global."

It should be evident by now that much in Kuma's works, especially in case of the smaller ones, is the result of his thorough knowledge of, admiration for, and ingenious adaptation or transformed continuation of, the time-honored modes of historic environmental cultures and arts. Thus, his architecture is not an indulgence in sentimentality or nostalgia. Yet, his buildings, not unlike their predecessors, cannot be appreciated instantly as some titillating spectacles; nor can they be reduced to some easy form of consumerist entertainment; they disclose their nuanced qualities, profound values, and meanings by stealth and continuously, that is to say, only in the time-delayed interactive human experience. They aspire to what might be termed as *slow-time architecture*. Altogether, Kuma's work demonstrates that he is committed as much to modernity as to Japanese traditions without mimicking either of them.

opposite, clockwise, from top left: Beijing Tea House, China, 2014; Ginzan Onsen Fujiya Ryokan, Obanazawa, Japan, 2006; Xinjin Zhi Museum of Wisdom, Chengdu, China, 2011; Momofuku Ando Center of Outdoor Training, Komoro, Japan, 2010; Under One Roof, Art-Lab of EPFL Campus, Lausanne, Switzerland, 2016; One Omotesando Office Building, Tokyo, 2004

following page, left; clockwise, from top left: Shizuku by Chef Naoko, Japanese Restaurant, Portland, OR, USA, 2016; Lotus House, Zushi, Japan, 2005; Opposite House Hotel, Beijing, China, 2008; Café of Nezu Art Museum, Tokyo, 2009

following page, right; clockwise, from top left: Tea House in Vancouver, Canada, 2017. Photo: Ema Peter; Marché, Community Market, Yusuhara, Japan, 2010; Hongkou SOHO Office Building, Shanghai, China, 2015; Sunny Hills Omotesando Cake Shop, Tokyo, 2013

Acknowledgments

There have been several persons whose contribution to this book's publication have been indispensable, and we the authors would like to acknowledge their parts in it with much appreciation.

First, Stephen Bloom, the current Chief Executive Officer of the Portland Japanese Garden was much supportive of the book's concept, and spearheaded its realization. He provided us with information and unlimited access to the Garden in order to experience it directly, allowing us to take all new photographs of the gardens and the Cultural Village during different seasons. For a better grasp of the subject matter, he also invited the book's editor and designer to visit the Garden, which strengthened the intentions of all parties toward a common goal. Sadafumi Uchiyama, the Garden Curator and core member of the project's design team, turned out to be also an endless source of information regarding thorough details of the new developments as much as the history of the Garden itself, offering insight with tremendous knowledge and expertise. Diane Durston, the Arlene Schnitzer Curator of Culture, Art, and Education, was the person who so graciously and with extensive detail described to us the new cultural programs, exhibitions, and key parts of the Garden's mission, in which she is still instrumental. Lisa Christy, the Chief External Affairs Officer, was however most directly involved in the book, reviewing the texts as well as the illustrative material several times, she made numerous corrections regarding facts and data, providing photographic material from the Garden's collection, while contributing to their descriptive captions. Many thanks to all four of them for their generous support and friendship.

Regarding our publisher Rizzoli International in New York, we are indebted to our editor, Douglas Curran. He guided the process of writing and editing the text with great patience and skill, and very much in a timely manner. He was also an important liaison between us and the designer of the book, making the collaboration smooth and productive. Very significantly, we wish to express our sincerest gratitude our book's New York–based designer, Takaaki Matsumoto, who was assisted by his collaborator Amy Wilkins. Their artistry, skill, and dedication to the book project was exceptional and we are as delighted with the result as, most certainly, the reader. Mr. Matsumoto not only made an excellent work with the design of the book but also gave suggestions regarding its internal organization. We want to thank both our editor and book designers for their substantial effort to the publication.

Finally, we thank Kengo Kuma and his office in Tokyo for their contribution: both for the delivery of the architecture, and to this book by way of the book's introduction, which succinctly elucidates the motivation for the design of the new Cultural Village.

175

View of the *Tsubo Niwa* in Tateuchi Courtyard seen from the Jane Stimson Miller Living Room of the Jordan Schnitzer Japanese Arts Learning Center. Photo: James Florio

Credits for Design and Construction of
the Portland Japanese Garden Cultural Village

DESIGN TEAM

Design Architect:

Kengo Kuma & Associates: Kengo Kuma (Principal in Charge); Balazs Bognar (Project Architect); Kimio Suzuki (Renderer); Toshiki Meijo, Takumi Saikawa, Makoto Shirahama (Advisers); Nicola Acquafredda, Boyce Postma, Spencer Anderson, Momo Ozawa (Interns)

Design Landscape Architect:

Sadafumi Uchiyama Landscape Architect: Sadafumi Uchiyama (Principal), Desirae Wood (Landscape Project Manager)

Architect of Record:

Hacker Architects: Jonah Cohen (Principal in Charge, Project Manager); Jake Freauff (Project Architect); Tyler Nishitani (Project Architect); Jennie Fowler (Interiors Lead); Maddy Freeman (Interiors); Sarah Post-Holmberg, Scott Barton Smith, Vijayeta Davda (Design Team)

Landscape Architect of Record:

Walker Macy: Chelsea McCann (Principal), Keriann Head (Landscape Architect), Tim Clemen (Landscape Architect), Doug Macy (Adviser)

Engineers:

Structural: KPFF Consulting Engineers—Anne Monnier (Principal in Charge), Josh Richards (Design Principal), Christopher Pitt (Project Manager), Katie Ritenour (Project Engineer)
Civil: KPFF Consulting Engineers—Matt Dolan, Danielle Pruett, Andrew Chung
Geotechnical: GRI—Mike Reed
Mechanical: PAE—Paul Schwer (Principal), Marc Brune, Tim Elley
Electrical: PAE—Robert Smith, Steve Diffenderfer
Plumbing: PAE—Andrew Comstock

Design Consultants:

Sustainability: Green Building Services—Beth Shuck, Webly Bowles
Lighting: Luma Lighting Design—Zach Suchara (Director of Design), Scott Kuyper
Retail design: EOA/Elmslie Osler Architect—Robin Osler (Principal), Chris Shelley, Joana Torres, Xinai Liang
Signage design: Anderson Krygier—Elizabeth Anderson (Principal), Abby-Sophia Alway
Acoustical: Listen Acoustics—Tobin Cooley
Metal roofing: Bassett Construction—Rodney Bassett
Envelope Consultant: RDH Building Science—Dave Young
Public Process: Bookin Group—Beverly Bookin (Principal), Chris Hagerman

CONSTRUCTION TEAM

General Contractor: Hoffman Construction Company—Cade Lawrence (Operations Manager), Joshua Faulkner (Superintendent), Derek Monson (Project Manager), Michael Carpenter (Project Engineer)

Craftsmen

Custom Japanese castle walls: Suminori Awata (Japan), with Matt Driscoll (O'Driscoll Stone), Kyle Schlagenhauf (Green Man Builders), Ed Lockett (Stone Sculptures), Dan Dunn (Alpine Boulder Company)
Custom interior wood screens and café ceiling: Takumi Company—Dale Brotherton
Custom main stepped seating and other carpentry: Straight Up Carpentry—Brian West, Devin Albert
Custom chestnut *naguri* main doors: Nakamura Sotoji Construction (Japan)—Yoshiaki Nakamura

SPECIAL MENTION

Owner Representative: Urban Resources—Randy Boehm, Larry Atchison, Megan Myers

Client Leads: Portland Japanese Garden—Stephen D. Bloom (CEO), Cynthia Haruyama (Deputy Director), Sarah MacDonald (Executive Assistant to CEO, Project Manager)

Special Project Oversight Committee (SPOC): Don Stastny, Doug Macy, William Hughes, Michael Ellena, Ed McVicker, Dorie Vollum, Dean Alterman, Kia Selley, Nancy Merryman, Stephen D. Bloom, Sadafumi Uchiyama, Diane Durston, Sarah MacDonald, Randy Boehm, Cade Lawrence, Derek Monson, Jonah Cohen, Balazs Bognar

SUPPLIERS AND FABRICATORS

Roofing

Metal: Pure+Freeform (USA) with DNP (Japan)
Vegetated "GreenBiz" ceramic panels: Komatsu Seiren (Japan)—Teruhiro Okuya, Atsushi Yamatake, Takuro Kamatani

Interior Finishes

Restroom floor and wall tile: Lixil/Inax (Japan)
Gallery fabric wall covering: Lixil/Kawashima Selkon (Japan)
All plumbing fixtures: DXV, American Standard (USA)

Furnishings

Executive reception furniture: Time & Style (Japan)—Ryoichi Satake, Masato Izumisawa
Library table: George Nakashima Woodworker (USA)
Library seating: Time & Style (Japan)—Ryoichi Satake, Masato Izumisawa
Café seating: Time & Style (Japan)—Ryoichi Satake, Masato Izumisawa
Exterior Benches: Studio 431 Landscape Forms (USA)